Louis
Braille

Betty Lou Kratoville

High Noon Books
Novato, California

Cover Design: Nanette Brichetto
Cover Photo: Pictorial History Research
Interior Illustrations: Damon Rarey

International Standard Book Number: 1-57128-143-6

10 09 08 07
1 0 9 8 7 6 5 4

Contents

CHAPTER 1

Early Days

In the past, life was very hard for the blind.
Parents who were poor often had no way to care
for a blind child. They sent their blind sons and
daughters to grim workhouses. Or simply turned
them out into the streets. In either case, the
children were starved and abused. And in most
cases, blind children died at an early age.

Schools? Why would one send a blind child
to school? How could they be taught? Who would
have the skills to teach them? It was found that

some blind children had amazing memories. They could remember every fact they heard. Why not teach them through their ears? Sadly, only a few schools were willing to try. And the results were not very good.

Few people know that Louis Braille was blind. He was born in a small French town in 1809. His sight was perfect when he was born. Louis had a good home. His father had a small shop. Here he made harnesses. His mother baked huge loaves of bread in her oven. What she grew in her garden went into a steaming kettle of soup. In the evenings she knitted warm socks for her four children. The Brailles led a simple life. But they were rich in their strong love for one another.

Louis did all of the things small French boys liked to do. He walked to the town well each day with his sister. Once a week he went to the market. Here the family sold leeks and cabbages from its garden.

The thing he liked best was to spend time in his father's harness shop. What a fine place it was! He watched his father cut through thick leather with a sharp knife. The town people liked their horses to look dashing. So Louis's brother spent his time making bright fringe and tassels. Three-year-old Louis often played with scraps of leather.

One day after lunch Louis walked into the shop. He planned to make a harness all by himself. How proud his father would be! Perhaps he would let Louis help in the shop.

The little boy reached for one of his father's pointed tools. Strictly forbidden, of course! Louis bent close to the piece of leather. How could he know that disaster was about to strike? The shop tool slipped from his hand. It went straight into Louis's left eye!

His screams brought his family on the run. What to do? An old woman lived in the town. She was thought to have healing powers. She came at once. She soaked a cloth in lily water. Then she placed it on Louis's bleeding eye.

The next day the Brailles took him to a doctor. There was not much this man could do.

He told them to keep cold cloths on the eye. Louis was to stay in a dark room.

In spite of good care, the eye got infected. And this spread to the right eye. Things began to blur. Then one terrible day Louis woke up in a dark world. He was completely blind!

CHAPTER 2

One Step at a Time

Louis had a close family. And many good friends in the town. Everyone wished to help the small blind boy. His mother guided his short fingers over objects in the house and yard. In this way he could "see" them.

Some things Louis learned by himself. He learned about the sound waves his steps made. If the sound waves hit a wall, they made one sound, If there was open space ahead, the sound was not the same. He learned to know friends and neighbors by their voices. He could even tell who owned the carts and wheelbarrows that passed by. He learned how many taps of his cane would take him to the well. Or to the stone bridge. Or to the village square.

He missed his young friends. Now and then one or two of them might stop in to say hello. But he couldn't run about or play their games. And so they would drift away. For the most part Louis's days were dull and lonely. He often sat in the sun in front of his house. The sun felt good on his face. And he could dream of what his life might have been.

Then one day the town church got a new priest. His name was Father Palluy. The priest liked Louis's quick smile. He was pleased with the way the boy got himself around the town. Louis had every right to be sad. But he seemed such a cheerful child.

"You have a fine boy there," he said to the Brailles.

"Yes," they agreed. "But we are worried. What is to become of him?"

"I would like to try to teach him," said Father Palluy.

The Brailles were happy with this offer. And so was Louis. Each day he tapped his way to the priest's house across the road from the church. Each day Father Palluy read him stories from the Bible. He told him about the wonders of nature.

8

Louis was thrilled by the beautiful music the priest played on the church organ. And, best of all, he gave Louis hope. He spoke of great people – blind, yes – but who still led good, rich lives.

Days flew by, and suddenly Louis was seven years old. Now the priest felt he had gone as far as he could with Louis. The boy should go to school.

Louis did his best at the small town school. The teachers tried hard to find ways to teach him. He could remember facts from one day to the next. He could do arithmetic problems in his head. His answers were quick and correct. But he could not read. And he could not write. What was to be done?

Once again his good friend Father Palluy had an answer. He had heard of a school for the blind in Paris. It was called the Royal Institute for the Blind. Here students were taught to read. To *read*! And to write! And to sew! And to play a musical instrument!

The Brailles looked at one another. It sounded wonderful. But how much would such a school cost? Father Palluy to the rescue! He took a trip to Paris. He talked to the head of the school about Louis. He brought back good news. The school would pay his fees! The Brailles were filled with joy! Their son could not believe his ears. But it was true.

A few weeks later Louis's clothes were

packed in a wooden box. With his box of clothes he took a stagecoach to Paris. A new life was about to begin. A life very different from the one he had known.He was ten years old, and the world was about to open up for him.

CHAPTER 3

The First Year in Paris

The Royal Institute was a tall grey stone building. It was old and chilly and damp. Sixty blind boys lived at the school. Louis was given a uniform. He struggled into scratchy woolen pants and jacket. He couldn't see himself. But he guessed he looked like all the other students.

The first night was the worst. He was shown a bed in a room with ten other boys. He was the youngest. The students were all kinds. But he was very, very homesick!

The thick books at the Royal Institute
were filled with raised capital letters.

Louis quickly learned that the teachers were strict. Boys who broke the rules were punished. Sometimes they were given only bread and water for their meals. Sometimes they were placed in a room to stay alone for days on end.

Of course, the school had its good points. But its books were not one of them. The Royal Institute had only 14 books! Each book weighed many pounds. They were placed on stands because they were too heavy to hold. The thick pages in the books were filled with raised capital letters. The students "read" these books by passing their fingers over the large letters. The letters were widely spaced. Yes, the boys learned to read. But it was at a snail's pace. It took Louis so long to come to the end of a sentence, sometimes he would have forgot its beginning! Worst of all, when a student left school, he could find no books with raised letters. So his reading was at an end.

Louis learned quickly. So quickly that in a short time he had read all 14 books. The teachers found other things for him to do. Besides his regular lessons he learned to knit. All of the students knitted slippers. These were sold to raise money for the school.

Louis found he could play the piano and organ by ear. Each day he spent hours in the music room. For field trips the students lined up along a rope. A teacher led the way. He told the students about the things they were passing. He helped them listen for new sounds.

Louis made his first friend. A friend who would last a lifetime. Gabriel had the bed next to Louis. They shared stories about their homes. Gabriel taught Louis to play checkers and chess. He showed him how to save bits of bread to feed pigeons in the school's yard. The boys were seldom apart. And Louis was no longer homesick.

No matter how damp the school was . . . No matter how strict its teachers . . . Louis loved it.

The year passed quickly. Soon it was July and time to go home. Two months to surprise his family with how much he had learned. Two months to smell the fresh country air. Two months to visit with Father Palluy and tell him all about the school. Two months to play the church organ for his friends in town.

And then back to school . . .

CHAPTER 4

Dots and Dashes

Louis was in his third year at the Royal Institute in Paris. By this time he was sure that the raised alphabet was not the best way for blind students to read and to learn. There had to be a better way. He didn't know what it was. He just knew that something had to be done.

One day the school had a guest. His name was Charles Barbier. He was a captain in the French army. The captain had solved a huge problem. His soldiers needed to read orders at night. They could not use their flashlights. This would show their enemies where they were. So Captain Barbier found a piece of heavy cardboard. On it he punched a code of dots and dashes with a pointed stylus. (A stylus is like a nail.) His men could read the raised "humps" by touch in the dark.

The captain's dots and dashes did not make words. They made the *sounds* that letters make. (Today we call that phonics.)

The head of the school called his staff and students together. He passed out samples of Captain Barbier's raised dots and dashes. Louis wanted to shout with joy. "This is it! This is it!" he told his friend Gabriel.

Everyone was eager to try this new method. The students spent hours punching out dots and dashes. Then they would try to read one another's notes. But what was this? One could not punch out numbers. How could one show a comma? Or a period? Or a question mark? And it took so many dots to make one word. Sometimes a simple sound needed 12 dots. No, there had to be a better way.

Yet Louis was sure that raised dots were the answer. But how? Sometimes he could not sleep. He would stay up all night. Perhaps dots placed this way would work. Perhaps dots placed that way. No! He must try again. After such nights he often fell asleep in class the next day.

In the summer months at home his mother worried about his bad cough. "You must get more rest, Louis," she would say. After a few weeks at home the cough was gone. But back at the damp school it returned – worse than ever. Louis didn't seem to notice it. His thoughts were on only one thing. There must be a way that the blind could read all the wonderful written works of the world. And one day he would find it!

CHAPTER 5

Breakthrough

The idea, when it did come, struck like lightning!
Of course! Captain Barbier's dots and dashes
stood for sounds. Why could the dots and dashes
not stand for *letters*? Not too many dots. Just
enough for a fingertip to cover. This meant no
more than six dots.

$$
\begin{array}{ccc}
1 & \bullet \ \bullet & 4 \\
2 & \bullet \ \bullet & 5 \\
3 & \bullet \ \bullet & 6 \\
\end{array}
$$

Louis called his six dots a "cell." And this

cell made up Louis's base. All letters would spring from it.

He began with the first four letters of the alphabet. The letter A was dot one. The letter B was dots one and two. The letter C, dots one and four; the letter D, dots one, four, and five. Louis decided that he did not need Captain Barbier's dashes.

After weeks of work Louis had formed his alphabet. His six-dot cell has been changed a bit through the years. But it is still very much like his first dazzling breakthrough. How old was Louis when the six-dot idea first came to him? He was fifteen!

The director of the Royal Institute was Dr.

Pignier. He sent for Louis.

"What is this new system of writing all the boys are speaking of?" he asked.

"I would be happy to show it to you," Louis said. "Please read something to me. Anything you like."

The director picked up a book and read out loud. Louis's fingers flew as he punched dots into a piece of cardboard with his stylus.

Dr. Pignier stopped reading. Louis passed his index finger over the dots he had raised. He read the passage back word for word.

The director could not believe what he had heard. "But this is amazing," he said. "Everyone must hear of it."

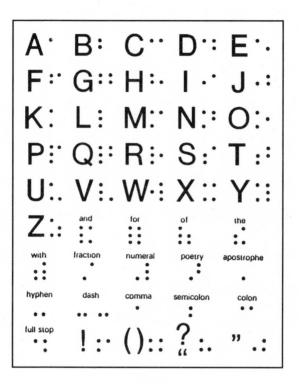

Braille Alphabet

He was true to his word. He went at once to see a man high in the French government. He showed samples of Louis's method. "This must be recognized as the only way to teach the blind," he insisted.

Nothing happened. Year after year Dr. Pignier made the same request. Year after year no change was made in teaching the blind. But no matter. Everyone at the Royal Institute was using Louis's raised dots!

Now Louis was seventeen. His school days were over. Dr. Pignier offered him a job as a teacher. Louis said yes. He loved the school. And his friend Gabriel would be teaching there, too.

Years passed. They were happy years. Louis

taught many school subjects from math to history. He found he could use the raised dot system for musical notes. Then he was able to teach piano and cello to his students.

He wrote textbooks. One was called "Methods of Writing Words, Music and Plain Songs by Means of Dots." His life was full and rich. The only cloud was his health. He worked too hard. Some days he had dizzy spells. His friends worried.

A high spot during those years was a visit from the king of France, Louis Phillip. The king came to the school with many important men. One of them was the Minister who had not liked Louis's alphabet years ago. Louis showed his dot alphabet to the king. The king asked questions about it. He smiled and nodded his head. So did the Minister. Louis's hopes grew high. Perhaps at long last people would learn about his six-dot cell. But he never heard from the king again.

Then one terrible day with no warning Dr. Pignier was fired! No one knew quite why. He had an assistant. His name was Dr. Dafau. This man was made director in Dr. Pignier's place.

Louis was upset. First of all, he had loved Dr. Pignier as a second father. Also, he was quite sure that Dr. Dafau did not like his raised-dot alphabet. Louis was right!

Then one terrible day with no warning Dr. Pignier was fired! No one knew quite why. He had an assistant. His name was Dr. Dafau. This man was made director in Dr. Pignier's place.

Louis was upset. First of all, he had loved Dr. Pignier as a second father. Also, he was quite sure that Dr. Dafau did not like his raised-dot alphabet. Louis was right!

CHAPTER 6

Banned Braille!

Dark days followed for Louis – and for the school. Dr. Dufau did not like the Braille system. He felt that it was too different. Besides, he did not like change of any kind.

"Everyone should use the same alphabet," he thundered. "The raised dots will set the blind apart. They will need their own teachers. Who will train these teachers? They will need their own books. Who will make these books? It won't work!"

The new director left nothing to chance. He searched the school from top to bottom. He gathered up every raised dot book, every stylus. Then he locked them in a closet.

Some of the teachers agreed with Dr. Dufau. Others did not agree. But they feared losing their jobs if they let their true feelings show. As a teacher, Louis dared not make his boss angry.

The students were quite another matter. They would not give up their raised dots. No stylus? They lent one another nails to punch dots. They kept their diaries in raised dots. They passed notes to one another in raised dots. Sometimes they were caught and punished. It didn't stop them. They kept right on punching dots and reading them with their fingertips. They were not about to give up this wonderful new chance to learn.

All this was a great strain on Louis. Once again his cough grew worse. He was thin and pale. He took a six-month leave of absence from the school and went home. Home was good medicine for him. His family's love, his mother's cooking, his many friends – all gave him new strength.

Gabriel wrote often. But he did not speak of Dr. Dufau. Louis wondered at this. But he put his worries aside. He must think only about getting well.

The country air did him good as it always

had. He went back to the Royal Institute in the fall. He was tan and fit. He had put on weight. He was still eager to teach. And he hoped to teach in raised dots. But his hopes were quickly dashed!

Things at the school could not have been worse. Now Dr. Dufau was burning raised-dot books. He refused to talk to anyone about them. His punishment for using them grew more strict. Some days it seemed as if the whole school was being punished!

Louis grew more depressed than he had ever been. He had done his best. What more could he do? He had no way of knowing that help was on the way.

It came in the form of one young man. His

name was Dr. Joseph Gaudet. He was the new assistant to Dr. Dufau. It did not take him long to see that students were using Braille's alphabet in secret. He set out to learn it himself. Only then would he know what the war between the students and Dr. Dufau was all about. He could not believe his eyes – or his fingertips.

"But this system is wonderful," he said to himself. "Why does Dr. Dufau not see this?"

He went straight to Dr. Dufau. The two men talked for a long time. At first Dr. Dufau would not change his mind. They talked some more.

"I have other things on my mind," Dr. Dufau said. "More important things. The school is falling down. We need a new building. I must raise money. Lots of money."

"All right," said Joseph Gaudet. "Raise your money. Put up your new building. I will wait. But not forever!"

CHAPTER 7

At Last – Victory!

The great day came. The new building was ready to open. There would be many changes. No more dark, damp rooms. Now all the classrooms and sleeping rooms were light and cheerful. At last girls could come to the school. It had a new name. It now was called the National Institute for Blind Youth.

A large crowd was there on opening day. Important men stood up and made long speeches. Gabriel and his students were in charge of singing

36

and music played by the school band.

At last Dr. Gaudet arose. He held a small booklet in his hand. It was called "Account of the System of Writing in Raised Dots for Use by the Blind." Gaudet had spent hours writing it. It told all about the raised-dot alphabet. It gave full credit to Louis Braille.

Dr. Gaudet finished reading the booklet aloud. Then it was time to show just how amazing the raised-dot alphabet was. Two blind students, a boy and a girl, were sent from the room. Another blind girl was led to the stage. A visitor was asked to read a poem to the girl. The visitor read slowly and clearly. The young girl used a stylus to punch holes in a sheet of thick

The blind boy was able to play the short piece of music perfectly.

paper. Then the girl who had been sent out of the room was asked to come back. She moved her fingers over the dots. She was able to read the poem without one error. Gasps of surprise rippled through the crowd.

Next, Dr. Gaudet asked another guest to hum a few bars of music. As the guest hummed, a blind teacher punched the notes into paper. Now the boy was called in. He was led to a piano. There he ran his fingers over the dots. He was able to play the short piece of music perfectly.

The crowd stood up and cheered. They called for the man who had invented this wonderful system. Louis went to the front of the hall. The people clapped and shouted his name. Never had he expected such a day. If only his family might have been there!

CHAPTER 8

The Last Years

For years Louis had not been strong enough to teach. He spent his days putting books into raised-dot form. He liked to play the piano and organ. He visited with Gabriel and other friends. He kept in touch with students who had left the school.

In 1847 a great surprise! A railroad was to be built between Paris and Strasbourg. It had to run straight through the land Louis owned in his home town. The French government was willing to pay a large sum if Louis would let the trains pass through his land.

Louis never dreamed of so much money! Now he could pay people to put books into raised dots. Now his goal of "many books all over France" was within reach.

These were the best days for Louis. He had lived at the school for 27 years. It was his "home." His friends there were his "family." It was a good life!

It was not to last. One bitter December day Louis caught a cold. He was put to bed, and he never rose again. On January 6, 1852, he died just two days after his 43rd birthday. His brother Simon and his good friends were at his bedside.

A wooden box was found in his room. It was marked "To be burned without opening." Friends opened it. It was filled with small rolls of paper each signed by Louis and a student. What did they mean? His friends looked at them more closely. Then they understood. The rolls showed how much money Louis had lent to his students. It was clear that he did not want the loans to be paid back.

———————

It did not happen all at once. But it did happen. Today Louis Braille's raised dots are used in every country in the world. Books, magazines, and newspapers are printed in Braille. Students have typewriters and computers that type in Braille.

Louis's home is now a museum. The very best tribute to him can be found on a plaque in front of the house.

In this house

on January 4, 1809

was born

Louis Braille

The inventor of the system of writing in

raised dots for use by the blind.

He opened the doors of knowledge to all

those who cannot see